BIRDS BUILD NESTS

Written by Yvonne Winer

Illustrated by Tony Oliver

i≈i Charlesbridge

Birds build nests
Secret and deep,
In holes in old trees
Or banks that are steep.
That's where birds build their nests.

Birds build nests
Where water birds wade.
Large floating rafts
In the lotus bloom's shade.
That's where birds build their nests.

Birds build nests
Tranquil and dark,
In old hollow trees
With rough, weathered bark.
That's where birds build their nests.

Birds build nests
On islands at sea.
Ocean rookeries for birds,
Wild and free.
That's where birds build their nests.

Birds build nests
Silhouetted up high,
Like magical castles
Perched in the sky.
That's where birds build their nests.

Birds build nests,
Eggs deep inside,
Secret spaces
Where fledgelings hide.
That's how birds build their nests.

Birds build nests
From mud, rich and brown,
Delicately lined with
Velvet and down.
That's how birds build their nests.

Birds build nests,
True tailors of old,
Stitching intricate patterns
Of russett and gold.
That's how birds build their nests.

Birds build nests,
Delicate, small . . .
A spider-web fantasy
Hidden from all.
That's how birds build their nests.

Birds build nests
On rough craggy peaks,
High in the mountains
Above valleys so deep.
That's where birds build their nests.

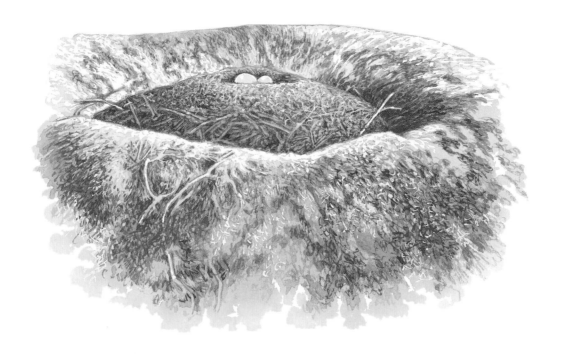

Birds build nests
In mounds that are warm,
Havens from predators,
Secure from all harm.
That's why birds build their nests.

Birds build nests
As waves splash the land.
Camouflaged eggs
Among sea shells and sand.
That's where birds build their nests.

Birds build nests
As spring comes once more.
Invisible hollows
On the vast tundra floor.
That's when birds build their nests.

Birds build nests

From morning 'til night,

Tireless weavers,

Designers in flight.

That's when birds build their nests.

Nest Identification Guide

There have been over nine thousand species of birds identified worldwide. Their nests vary from the most amazing delicate hidden pouches made from spiderwebs and lichen to vast tower-like stick structures on telegraph poles, steeples and cliff ledges. Other nests are no more than shallow hollows in the ground.

Birds are clever architects that design their nests to protect their eggs and young, often in underground tunnels, meticulous mud homes or floating rafts. From the way they build their nests, we see that some birds live in large sociable communities. Other birds may never build their own homes. Instead, they sneak their eggs into the nests of other species. The following identification guide describes some of the diverse nests birds build around the world.

The birds' nests in this identification guide are arranged in the same order as they appear on the pages of this book, beginning on the cover and title page with the ruby-throated hummingbird. The small drawing in the left margin is a miniature of the drawing above each poem.

Ruby-Throated Hummingbird
Archilochus colubris
United States

This is the only hummingbird that breeds east of the Mississippi river, from southern Canada to the Gulf coast, and winters mainly in the tropics. These tiny birds are particularly attracted to red flowers such as salvia, trumpet creeper, and hibiscus. Hummingbirds are the only birds that can fly backwards and hover in one spot like insects. They lay two white eggs in a woven nest of plant down held together with spider silk and decorated with lichens.

Spotted Pardalote
Pardalotus punctatus
Australia

These small birds have short tails, strong legs, and stout blunt bills. They nest in holes in earth banks, dug usually by the male. He loosens soil with his bill and moves it back to the entrance then swiftly kicks it a few inches beyond. The nest, a domed structure of bark fragments, is then constructed at the end of the tunnel which may be one to two feet deep.

Lotus Bird
Irediparra gallinacea
Southern Philippines, Eastern Indonesia, New Guinea, Northern & Eastern Australia

Preferring tropical and sub-tropical freshwater swamps and lagoons, the lotus bird favours extensive, deep, and permanent wetlands. Its long legs are ideal for wading, and elongated toes and claws help it walk on floating vegetation such as waterlilies. The lotus bird builds shallow nests on floating platforms made from the leaves of water plants.

Laughing Kookaburra
Dacelo novaeguineae
Australia

This bird is common in eastern Australia. It is a clever and persistent predator, hunting prey from a strategic perch. The kookaburra is found in open eucalypt forest, open rainforest, parks, and suburban gardens. Its call is a loud chuckling laugh, often in chorus with other members of its family. The nest is usually no more than an unlined hollow in a tree, where two to four smooth, white, rounded eggs are laid.

Great Cormorant
Phalacrocorax carbo
Worldwide

This bird prefers a habitat that includes extensive permanent water. Its diet of fish is supplemented by crabs, frogs, and large insects. Unlike other cormorants, it does not stay long underwater when diving for fish. The great cormorant breeds in colonies that range from a few to about two thousand pairs. The large stick nest may be re-used several times. These nests are usually in trees over water and often appear in the same area as ibis, egret, and other water birds' nests.

White Stork
Ciconia ciconia
Europe, Turkey, Iraq, Iran, Tunisia, North Africa

The white stork generally builds its nest on chimneys, rooftops, or in trees. It adds to the nest every year, creating a huge structure. It lays three to six eggs from which only three chicks may reach maturity. Adult birds are very attentive parents, shielding their young from bad weather and other storks.

Red-winged Blackbird
Agelaius phoeniceus
North & Central America

Primarily a marsh bird, the red-winged blackbird will nest near any body of water. It raises two or three broods a season and then joins other blackbirds in flocks that can number hundreds of thousands. The nest is built by the female and consists of sedge leaves, rushes, grasses, rootlets, and mosses bound to surrounding vegetation with milkwood fibers and lined with fine grasses.

Fairy Martin
Cecropis ariel
Australia

This bird is an accomplished builder, adept at repairing damaged nests and making new ones using many pellets of mud. They nest in large groups. As many as seven hundred nests have been found in one colony. Apart from using rock overhangs and caves, they also use man-made structures such as bridges, culverts, and drains to shelter their nests.

Long-tailed Tailor Bird
Orthotomus sutorius
India, Southern China, Malaysia

This bird bends a large green leaf or several smaller leaves into a sort of cup, then, using its beak as a needle, it pierces holes in the edges and sews the leaves together by drawing threads, such as plant fibres or silk from spiders' webs, through the holes. It then builds its nest of plant or animal-down inside this cup.

Rufous Fantail
Rhipidura rufifrons
Indonesia, New Guinea, Solomon Islands, and Australia

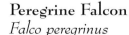

The rufous fantail lives in dense forest, open timber, and urban areas. Its beautifully constructed 'wine-glass' nest is a compact cup of fine grass bound with spiders' webs. The nest has a tail of grass that trails about five inches.

Peregrine Falcon
Falco peregrinus
All continents except Antarctica

The peregrine falcon is a powerful predator that hunts other birds in flight. It does not build a nest. The eggs are laid in a shallow scrape in a ledge of a cliff or even on a well-placed skyscraper. Sometimes it takes over the stick nest of another species, and the same nest may be used for hundreds of years.

Mallee Fowl
Leipoa ocellata
Australia

This bird lives in the dry mallee scrubs of southern Australia. The male builds and tends the incubation mound, which consists of a hole filled with vegetation and covered with sand. The mound may reach sixteen feet in diameter and four feet high. The female lays from five to thirty-three eggs in the mound, which keeps the eggs at a constant temperature.

Little Ringed Plover
Charadrius dubius
Europe, Africa, Asia, North Australia

The most widely distributed of the small, sand-colored plovers, the little ringed plover nests on the sandy shores of lakes, ponds, and rivers. The nesting hollow contains four small eggs practically indistinguishable from the pebbles with which it is lined. Both male and female birds take turns incubating the eggs.

Snowy Owl
Nyctea scandiaca
Arctic region

Snowy owls breed in the vast, level, treeless tundra of the lands surrounding the North Pole. Lemmings are the mainstay of their diet, and in years when these are scarce, the snowy owl either does not nest at all or lays only three or four eggs compared with double this number when food is plentiful.

Golden Weaver
Ploceus subaureus
Africa

The male golden weaver plays the dominant role in nest building. The nest, woven of grass, straw, and vegetable fibers, is generally suspended from the thinnest branches of a thorny Acacia tree. False nests are sometimes built in an effort to protect the eggs and brood from egg-eating snakes. Weaver birds are so named because of their instinctive ability to build their nests by weaving together grass, straw, stems, and other vegetable fibers. These small, social birds are found on the plains, savannahs, and forests of Africa.

Dedication
In memory of my father-in-law, Sid Winer
I was touched by his vast knowledge and love of birds.
Also, to David Lester who shares his enthusiasm for,
and knowledge of, birds with Kari and Bonnie.

Acknowledgements
To Jennifer Woodman, who provided so much
editorial assistance in the early drafts of all my books,
for her friendship and support.

References
The Life of Birds by David Attenborough. New Jersey, Princeton University Press, 1998
Birds for All Seasons by Jeffery Boswall. London, BBC Publications, 1986
The Audubon Society Field Guide to North American Birds, Eastern Region by John L Bull. New York, Knopf, 1994
Bird Behaviour by Robert Burton. London, Granada, 1986
Birds' Eggs and Nests by Jan Hanzák. New York, Hamlyn, 1971
Illustrated encyclopedia of birds by Jan Hanzák and Jirî Formañek. London, Octopus Books, 1977
Eastern Birds' Nests (Peterson North American Field Guides) by Hal H. Harrison. New York, Houghton Mifflin, 1998
Honeyeaters and their Allies of Australia; The National Photographic Index of Australian Wildlife
by Wayne Longmore. Sydney, Angus & Robertson, 1991
Field Guide to Australian Birds by Michael Morcombe. Archerfield, Queensland, Steve Parrish Publishing, 2000
Roberts' Birds of Africa, 6th edition, by Austin Roberts. London, New Holland, 1993
Extraordinary Animals of the World by Marcus Schneck. London, New Burlington Books, 1990
Cuckoos, Nightbirds and Kingfishers of Australia; The National Photographic Index of Australian Wildlife,
by Ronald Strahan. Sydney, Angus & Robertson, 1994

Internet Resources
Yahoo Birding:
http://dir.yahoo.com/recreation/outdoors/birding/
An extensive list of links to bird sites.
Bird Pictures:
http://www.yahooligans.com/Downloader/Pictures/School_Bell/Science___Nature/Animals/Birds/
A site with hundreds of free downloadable bird pictures and links to other bird photo sites.
Electronic Resources on Ornithology:
http://www.chebucto.ns.ca/Environment/NHR/bird.html
A comprehensive list of links to other bird sites.
Birding:
http://www.birding.about.com/hobbies/birding/mbody.htm
An interesting site with information and links on all aspects of birds and bird watching.
Classroom Feeder Watch:
http://www.birds.cornell.edu/cfw/
Cornell University's project site that focuses on the habits of birds at a feeder.

First American Edition, 2002
Published by Charlesbridge Publishing
85 Main Street, Watertown. MA 02472
(617) 926-0329 / www.charlesbridge.com
Text copyright © 2001 by Yvonne Winer. Illustrations coyright © Tony Oliver, 2001.

First published by Margaret Hamilton Books in 2001.
This edition is published under license from Margaret Hamilton Books, a division of Scholastic Australia Pty. Limited.

Library of Congress Cataloging-in-Publication Data is available upon request.

ISBN 1-57091-500-8 (reinforced for library use). ISBN 1-57091-501-6 (softcover)

Printed in Singapore by Tien Wah Press.
(hc) 10 9 8 7 6 5 4 3 2 1
(sc) 10 9 8 7 6 5 4 3 2 1
The illustrations in this book were done in watercolors.
Typeset in Bernhard.